How to Write an Essay

Lucy Xiang-fu Wainger

RED MARE
PRESS

HOW TO WRITE AN ESSAY

Edited by Elyssia Nguyen and Sara Dudo.

Cover design by Emelie Mano.

Interior design by Julianne Johnson.

Red Mare Press / Discover New Art, LLC
70 SW Century Drive, Suite 100442, Bend, Oregon 97702

www.redmarepress.com

Red Mare Press is a division of Discover New Art, LLC.
The Red Mare Press name and logo are trademarks of
Discover New Art, LLC.
The publisher is not responsible for websites (or their content) that are not owned by the publisher.

ISBN 979-8-9939024-3-2

Printed in the United States of America.

CONTENTS

Essay on My Education

In my senior seminar on Emily Dickinson, I sought to write
my final paper on the so-called "Master Letters."

(In my freshman year of high school, my English teacher wondered
why her students could refer to Angelou, Bishop, Collins, but not
Dickinson—only Emily. Afterward, I never called her anything else.)

When I read the Letters, read *I used to think if I died –*
I could see you – so I died as fast as I could – , I thought perhaps
the tightening in my muscles could be the basis for a paper
and not for longing, nor despair.

I had a thesis. I cannot now recall it.

On the plane to visit my *Bright Absentee!* I thumbed my used copy
of the *Collected* (Johnson's edition), dutifully noted the poems
I felt vibrating at the same frequency as the Letters.

(If my life has strings, they are not bound to anything isolable.
Deep sea eruptions belch waves to rock the puny boat of the self.)

I could not abide the swampy library air. To research, I turned off
the lights and lay under the covers, laptop screen at maximum
brightness. What was my thesis? That should desire destroy me,
no one will remain to find my notes beneath the bed.

I skimmed scholarly articles on themes of masochism, submission,
dissolution in Emily's poems, articles that enclosed their subjects'
with vast, sweeping arms. The phrase "under-theorized" haunted me.

How exactly is one to theorize a feeling which undoes mastery,
begs to be Mastered by someone, something other than the self?

(In high school, I knew a girl who wrote an assignment
saying she is a collector. She puts things into piles
and puts those piles into drawers and then she waits.)

Chasing links in the dark, I found myself reading an ethnography
of a BDSM community (urban, mostly white) by a woman who,
to conduct her research, entered their world as a submissive.

I had a thesis, but what I remember best is an image:
the ethnographer was invited to play with a veteran dominant—
an honor. She removed her top and faced the Saint Andrew's cross,
not wanting to expose her breasts to the crowd.

He hit her, and her back lit up. He hit her again. He kept hitting her
and this is what I remember: eventually she turned, no longer
self-conscious, just desperate to protect her burning back.

But since Myself – assault Me –
How have I peace
Except by subjugating
Consciousness?

Here is what I learned in college: the great poems survive
extraction from time, place, attachment. The great writers
survive as thin black text on the translucent pages
of a literature textbook I rented last semester.

What survives in my memory?

The girl from my high school who wrote that she is a collector.

An ethnographer pressing her burnt back
to the soothing surface of a Saint Andrew's cross.

The tightening in my muscles upon discovering the letters
Emily did not write for me to read.

Handbook

I used to know her. The word for what she collected is *things*. What were the things? Fringed, and often dark blue. Often untetherable. Once the things had accumulated, acquired the singular status of *pile*, she'd put the pile in a drawer. Then she'd wait.

I pause here. I reference my files and am distracted by someone in the hot knit of realizing, however many years ago, and for the first time. I enjoy these backward jaunts, sterile as they are; I enjoy tracing the elbows on which people hinge.

The collector, for instance, first encountered the word *inculcated* on the damp November sands of Coney Island. She rode her train to its end, book underarm, her belly a tangle of eels. How do I know? Because she put it in, all of it—the book's damp tangle, the word springing forth full-bodied and unbearable.

She waited. Now she is elsewhere. I busy myself pulling attempts from my collection, attempts by children to pinpoint the moment when whatever they were made of grew whole enough to walk away from.

Data or a Feeling

I am on the hunt for axioms.

My methods are flawed,
my reasoning motivated by the crowd
of fish nibbling my feet.

Give them something tangible, writes
my student, *like data or a feeling.*

Thick, dripping slabs of data.

I carry a ball of twine in my backpack,
I carry my backpack everywhere.

Like any mammal,
my professor encourages
the use of concrete examples.

Flakes of fact turning in the light.

At the end of the hall: a door. Behind it,
a bed someone's already slept in.

The compound wound of the eye.
The nervous system, illiterate.

Maybe I'd recognize you on the train.

When the air inside my lungs equals
the air outside my body—
that's how I'll say it's real.

Attempt for the Time Being

*Wow. I'm really going to miss you. It's crazy, I know, since you don't
even exist yet. And unless you find this book and start to read, maybe
you never will.*

Ruth Ozeki

The girl catching up to herself
writes: *Now!*

What now feels like: a letter
without address, hoping to mean
by the time it gets there.

Today my freshman composition students deal with audience. I tell
them the reader they want to reach shapes the text they'll create, the
choices they'll make in the process. Need inside you corresponds with
need inside me—makes me spit out these words in this order.

One of my students says her audience is everyone. Not because
everyone listens. Because anyone could overhear.

The girl catches up to herself
        in the stairwell smelling of formaldehyde,

between the lines of a geometry worksheet,
shuffling down the interminable hallway,
crouched over the middle stall toilet.
The bathroom mirror, scuffed and smudged
        like a subway window, renders her
                a caricature. She returns
to class, meets nobody's eyes.

Some texts use *you* as a ruse—creates the appearance of distance
within a sealed loop: the one speaking and the one addressed are one,
are one. The reader is reduced to eavesdropper.

Such texts leave no room for *you* proper, yet you remain. What keeps
you there?

Currency in one age equals relic in another,
a museum exhibit yawned and slid past.

Impossible to transmit any fixed insight,
any warning. I've sent my future selves

uncountable messages, lessons packaged
in the least perishable language I've got—

I am quaint to them. I know now: knowing
never lasts. Leaves a chitinous remainder.

During the Q&A, the novelist says you cannot physically bring yourself to write unless you have some faith in a future—the barest expectation that eventually, there will be a reader. At least one. Without this the body in impotence will rebel, won't pick up the pencil or tap at the keys.

I am writing, so there must lie somewhere in my body the expectation of a future reader, however frail. What I have to do now is keep from crushing it.

ৼ

The girl needs you. Can you hear me?

She's in the apartment stairwell, glancing up and down
at blank blue space to fall through.

She's writing a word on her thigh with a knife.

She's arranging a grid of pills, TV on,
cartoons blaring theme songs to no one.

She's counting the last few minutes. Thinking
not about you.
   Are you there?
   We need her.

ৼ

In ancient Mesopotamia, the earliest writing tracked transaction and debt, ensured what was owed had been or would be paid. Information extruded from the scribe's body, left the semantic guarantors of gesture, tone, eye contact, fist, and entered wilderness. Simultaneously,

an audience—creditor, bureaucrat—awaited objective measurements
that did not yet exist.

Chicken and egg: to write, I must believe in you; in reading, you
assemble me.

The girl wrote to me once, though she didn't know it.
In a hospital bed, she puked up liquid charcoal

then tried to do her English homework: finish reading
Oedipus Rex, the primal scene between seeing and blindness.

Three lines from Ode IV jutted from the text, pricking
her mind's numb surface. She couldn't explain why

she reached for her notebook, wrote down the lines.
The pencil was dull. The words could've been anyone's.

She went back to her reading, and years passed.

I and you and she are relative terms, spatial signifiers. If the frame
of reference shifts, so do our positions' coordinates. I am only I for
myself; I live so many other lives in the clothes of you, even more in
those of she.

The view slips, but I am standing here. I am still standing right here.

I no longer know whether you stand behind me or ahead.

Yanhuitlán

I'm not well Lola I almost never dream.

Roberto Bolaño

She took a photo—not of me—but with me in it.
Bricklaid curvature swells the red roof
with breastlike mounds. That's me at the highest point—
looming like an ant—a black stitch fastening
El Templo to backdrop mountain, the sky a silver threat.
Panoramic, the image stretches rightward
in grotesque simulation, melting the roof's hard edge,
the city sagging below the belly of the moon.
I don't remember how we got there—or how we left—
but I imagine she saw me not seeing her
and decided to capture it, as a conqueror creates
artifacts of belief, renders worlds falsifiable,
so in years hence her memory of us would remain
pristine as a mussel sucked from its shell.

Great Books

The four walls of your office define a space between spaces

Am I as you see me or is it the other way around

Bathroom paper towels spread across your desk
I can make us turkey sandwiches

Penelope's power was delay, warfare in miniature

You show me that when I cut class to cry out for an answer

Rabid and bereft, bridled by rotting need
I can't stand the breathing between us

Then your pile of blue ribbons gives my own face back to me
A shape that withstands the flux of other days

Which one of us wrote this page?

I know it was you who forgave that promise
some earlier self left me to keep

How to Write an Essay: A Practical Guide for the High School English Classroom

Read. *You have to have in you some cell, some gene, some germ that will vibrate in answer to sensations that you can neither define, nor dismiss,* said Nabokov, and you do. Cut out every word, sentence, paragraph that elicits such a vibration within you. Pile your cutouts like so many raked leaves. Then wait. The waiting is crucial. Pick a leaf at random from the pile and place it somewhere—not the center—of an empty table. Pick through the remaining leaves until you find one which, if you listen closely enough, you can hear crying out to the original leaf. Place the new leaf somewhere on the table where the two can hear each other. Repeat this with the new leaf, the remaining pile. Repeat until you have run out either of leaves or of responses to calls. The spaces between leaves, sticky with breathing—that's where you look for your essay.

But perhaps you do not wish to mutilate the pile of paper and glue which forms a book: fair enough. Nabokov also said a book is never read, only reread. A rereading of his words: that reading depends upon multiple readers—multiple versions of yourself distinct in time and therefore in habits of mind, in memories of pain, in familiarity with the book and its vernacular. A quick and dirty trick: to substitute the multiplicity generated by time with that by space. That is: document class discussion, your peers' impressions and insights into the book, whether by furiously transcribing what they say (or only those remarks that elicit a vibration) or by recording the session with a discreetly-placed smartphone. When it is time, pick the remark that feels most startling, most outlandish—but not false or indefensible— to your own thinking. Reconstructing the logic that bridges your thinking and your classmate's, or theirs and the book's, will form the feet of your essay.

When I refer to the reconstruction of logic, I do mean in the mathematical sense. In the same way we take as fact certain well-defined binary operations in order to speak of the integers, we take as fact not only the book's substance but also our own spontaneous impressions of it (inevitably stained by time, space, and self). Having withstood the scrutiny necessary to weed out superficial reactions, undesirable biases, and the like, such impressions are not a matter for debate; they are simply the third thing borne of book and body making contact as reactants. The method of the essay, therefore, is axiomatic: given the facts of the body, the book, and the third thing, what follows? Often, what follows looks very different from what was given. The strangest pleasure is to arrive at the conclusion wondering how on earth you reached it.

At times these methods will not work. At times the mind lies fallow. When all else fails, ask yourself: *where do I hurt in relation to this book?* If you start where it hurts, you might not always end there.

NOTES

"Essay on My Education" takes a line from Emily Dickinson's third "Master Letter" (L233, ca. 1861) and two lines from her poem "Me from Myself—to Banish—" (J642/Fr709, ca. 1862).

"Attempt for the Time Being" takes its epigraph from Ruth Ozeki's novel *A Tale for the Time Being* (2013). The account of writing's origins is from Alberto Manguel's *A History of Reading* (1997).

"Yanhuitlán" takes its epigraph from Roberto Bolaño's poem "Lola Paniagua" (trans. Laura Healy, 2007).

"How to Write an Essay: A Practical Guide for the High School English Classroom" takes a line and paraphrases another from Vladimir Nabokov's *Lectures on Literature* (1980). The italicized question in the final stanza belongs to Eda Tse.

ACKNOWLEDGMENTS

b l u s h: "Data or a Feeling"

Thank you to Dara Barrois/Dixon, Colin Drohan, Peter Gizzi, Elyssia Nguyen, Rachelle Toarmino, and Ocean Vuong for help in shaping these poems, and to Eric Grossman for supplying the big ideas.